A Savanna Habitat

Introducing Habitats

Bobbie Kalman and Rebecca Sjonger

Crabtree Publishing Company

www.crabtreebooks.com

Created by Bobbie Kalman

Dedicated by Robert Wainio
To papa's three girls, Mikaela, Alyssa, and Kaitlyn

Editor-in-Chief
Bobbie Kalman

Writing team
Bobbie Kalman
Rebecca Sjonger

Substantive editor
Kelley MacAulay

Project editor
Michael Hodge

Editors
Molly Aloian
Kathryn Smithyman

Design
Margaret Amy Salter
Samantha Crabtree
 (cover and series logo)

Production coordinator
Heather Fitzpatrick

Photo research
Crystal Foxton

Special thanks to
Jack Pickett and Karen Van Atte

Illustrations
Barbara Bedell: pages 19, 32 (top)
Katherine Kantor: pages 12, 14, 15 (grass), 18, 24, 32 (middle)
Bonna Rouse: pages 15 (roots), 22
Margaret Amy Salter: page 16

Photographs
© Richard Sobol/Animals Animals - Earth Scenes: page 23
Bruce Coleman Inc.: Peter Davey: page 29
© Peter Johnson/Corbis: page 17
iStockphoto.com: Muriel Lasure: page 13
© Torsten Brehm/naturepl.com: page 27
Photo Researchers, Inc.: Jacques Jangoux: page 16
Other images by Corel, Creatas, Digital Stock, Digital Vision,
 Photodisc, and Weatherstock

Library and Archives Canada Cataloguing in Publication

Kalman, Bobbie, date.
 A savanna habitat / Bobbie Kalman & Rebecca Sjonger.

(Introducing habitats)
ISBN-13: 978-0-7787-2952-5 (bound)
ISBN-13: 978-0-7787-2980-8 (pbk.)
ISBN-10: 0-7787-2952-4 (bound)
ISBN-10: 0-7787-2980-X (pbk.)

 1. Savanna ecology--Juvenile literature. I. Sjonger, Rebecca
II. Title. III. Series.

QH541.5.P7K343 2006   j577.4'8   C2006-904123-7

Library of Congress Cataloging-in-Publication Data

Kalman, Bobbie.
 A savanna habitat / Bobbie Kalman & Rebecca Sjonger.
  p. cm. -- (Introducing habitats)
 ISBN-13: 978-0-7787-2952-5 (rlb)
 ISBN-10: 0-7787-2952-4 (rlb)
 ISBN-13: 978-0-7787-2980-8 (pb)
 ISBN-10: 0-7787-2980-X (pb)
 1. Savanna ecology--Juvenile literature. I. Sjonger, Rebecca. II. Title.
III. Series.

QH541.5.P7K352 2007
577.4'8--dc22
                                              2006023328

Crabtree Publishing Company

www.crabtreebooks.com   1-800-387-7650
Copyright © **2007 CRABTREE PUBLISHING COMPANY**. All rights reserved. No part of this publication may be reproduced, stored in a retrieval system or be transmitted in any form or by any means, electronic, mechanical, photocopying, recording, or otherwise, without the prior written permission of Crabtree Publishing Company. In Canada: We acknowledge the financial support of the Government of Canada through the Book Publishing Industry Development Program (BPIDP) for our publishing activities.

Published in Canada
Crabtree Publishing
616 Welland Ave.
St. Catharines, ON
L2M 5V6

Published in the United States
Crabtree Publishing
PMB16A
350 Fifth Ave., Suite 3308
New York, NY 10118

Published in the United Kingdom
Crabtree Publishing
White Cross Mills
High Town, Lancaster
LA1 4XS

Published in Australia
Crabtree Publishing
386 Mt. Alexander Rd.
Ascot Vale (Melbourne)
VIC 3032

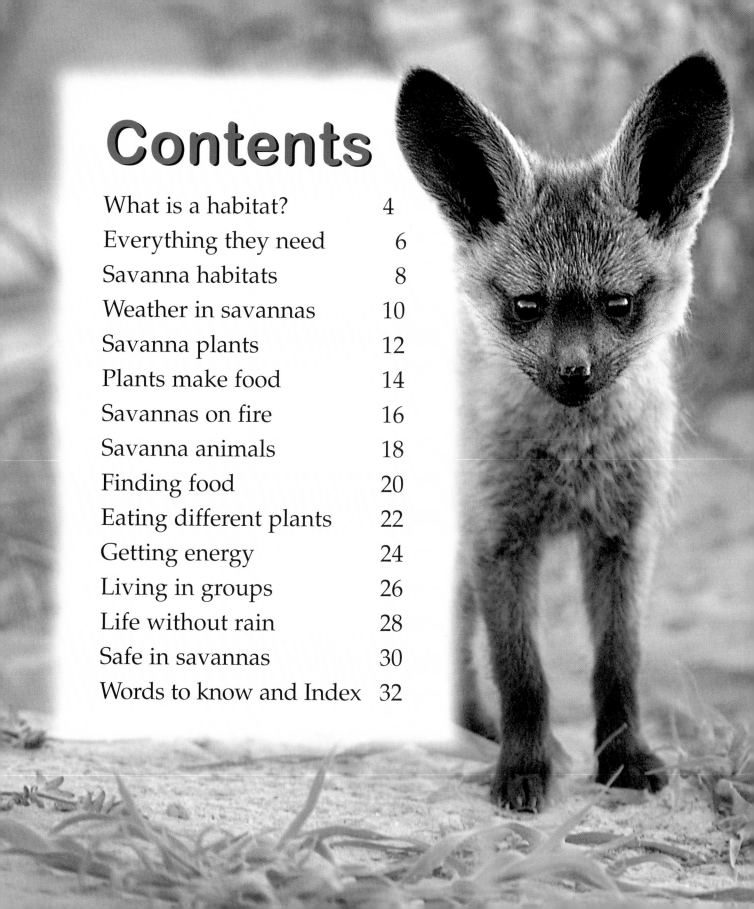

Contents

What is a habitat?   4
Everything they need   6
Savanna habitats   8
Weather in savannas   10
Savanna plants   12
Plants make food   14
Savannas on fire   16
Savanna animals   18
Finding food   20
Eating different plants   22
Getting energy   24
Living in groups   26
Life without rain   28
Safe in savannas   30
Words to know and Index   32

What is a habitat?

A **habitat** is a place in nature. Plants live in habitats. Animals live in habitats, too. These animals are cheetahs. Some animals make homes in their habitats.

Living and non-living things

There are **living things** in habitats. Plants and animals are living things. There are also **non-living things** in habitats. Rocks, water, and dirt are non-living things. These hippopotamuses spend a lot of time in water.

Everything they need

Living things need air, water, and food to stay alive. Plants and animals find everything they need in their habitats. These zebras found water to drink in their habitat.

Homes in habitats

These meerkats have made a home in their habitat. Meerkats make homes under the ground. Their homes are called **burrows**.

Savanna habitats

Savannas are habitats. They are large areas of land that are covered with grasses. The land is mainly flat. Some savannas have a few trees and **shrubs**. Shrubs are bushes.

African savannas

Savannas are found in many
places on Earth. This book
is about savannas in Africa.
African savannas are huge!

Weather in savannas

The weather in savannas is always hot. Savannas are also dry for most of the year. Sometimes it does not rain for several months.

Welcome water!
In summer, it rains in savannas. During storms, the rain falls, and strong winds blow. Lightning flashes in the sky. Loud thunder follows the lightning.

11

Savanna plants

Huge parts of savannas are covered with grasses. Small shrubs grow in some places. The shrubs grow close to the ground. They do not grow close together. There is not enough water in savannas for a lot of shrubs to grow in one place.

Water savers

Most kinds of trees cannot grow in savannas because savannas are too dry. Baobab trees grow in savannas. When it rains, baobab trees store water in their trunks. They use up the water during the months when it does not rain.

Plants make food

acacia tree

Living things need food to stay alive. Plants make their own food. They make food using sunlight, air, and water. Making food from sunlight, air, and water is called **photosynthesis**. This acacia tree makes its own food!

14

Parts for making food

A plant gets sunlight through its leaves. It also gets air through its leaves. The plant gets water through its roots. The plant uses sunlight, air, and water to make food.

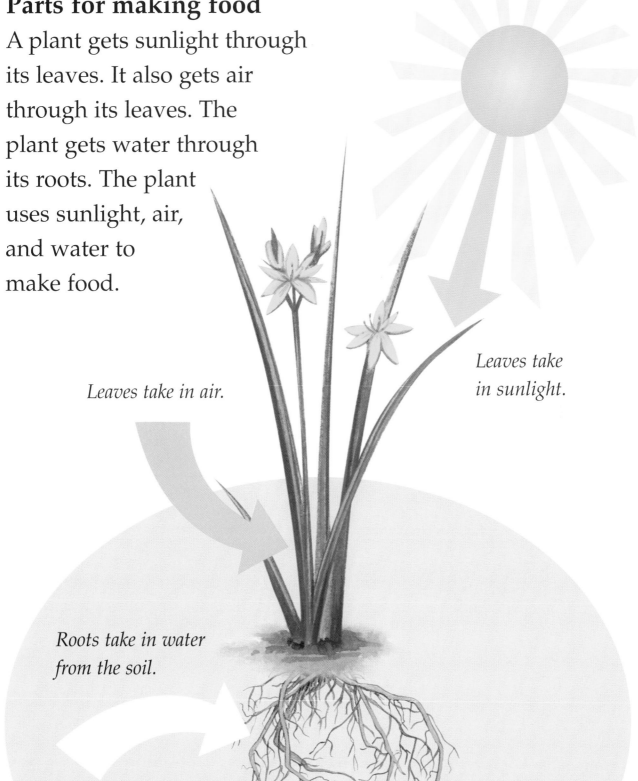

Leaves take in sunlight.

Leaves take in air.

Roots take in water from the soil.

Savannas on fire

The grasses in savannas are very dry. They catch fire easily. There are often fires in savannas. Lightning starts some of the fires. People start other fires. The fires kill many savanna plants.

Life goes on

Some savanna plants stay alive in the fires. Grasses stay alive because they have long roots. Fires do not burn the roots. When it rains, new grasses grow from the roots. These nyala are eating new grasses.

Savanna animals

This spring hare is the same color as brown grass. Its color hides it from other animals.

These animals live in a savanna. A savanna is their habitat. The animals find food and water in the savanna. They also find homes in the savanna.

These rhinoceros eat a lot of grass!

This gazelle can run away from lions.

The bat-eared fox has big ears. It can hear well.

This hyena eats the food that other animals leave behind.

This secretary bird has long legs. It can run quickly.

19

Finding food

Some of the animals that find
food in savannas are **herbivores**.
Herbivores eat only plants. A
rhinoceros is a herbivore. It eats
grasses and other plants.

Eating animals

Some savanna animals are **carnivores**. Carnivores eat animals. This crocodile is a carnivore. It eats fish and birds.

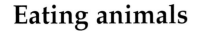

Eating both

Some savanna animals are **omnivores**. Omnivores eat both plants and animals. This ostrich is an omnivore. It eats grasses, leaves, and seeds. It also eats insects.

21

Eating different plants

Many savanna animals are herbivores or omnivores. These animals eat different kinds of plants. They also eat different parts of the plants. If all the animals ate the same parts of the same plants, the animals would soon run out of food!

Food for all

Some animals can reach plants that grow high above the ground. A giraffe can reach leaves that grow high on a tree. Other animals eat plants that they find on the ground. A baboon eats tall grasses. These baboons are eating grasses.

Getting energy

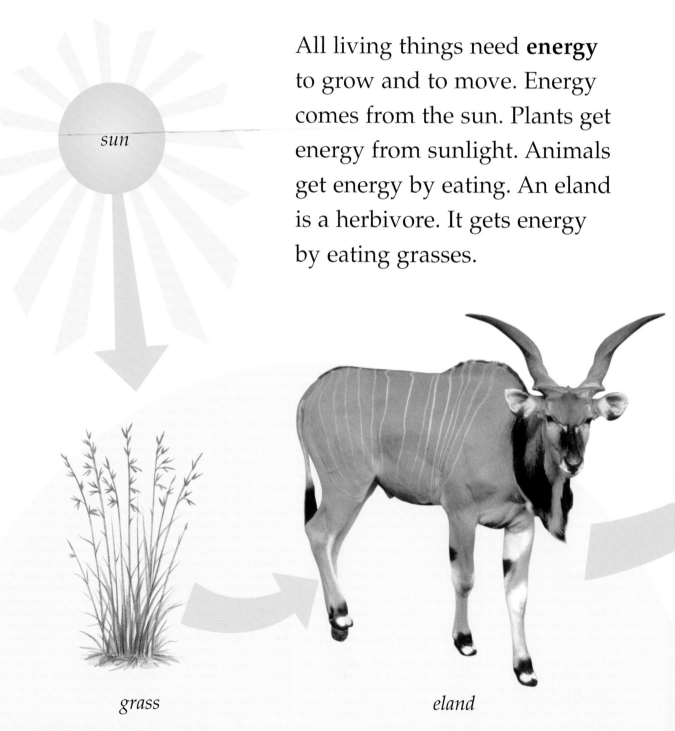

All living things need **energy** to grow and to move. Energy comes from the sun. Plants get energy from sunlight. Animals get energy by eating. An eland is a herbivore. It gets energy by eating grasses.

sun

grass

eland

cheetah

Carnivores get energy

Carnivores get energy by eating
animals. A cheetah is a carnivore.
It gets energy by eating an eland.

25

Living in groups

Many savanna animals live in groups. Wildebeests and zebras live in big groups called **herds**. Elephants and lions live in smaller groups. There are only four lions in this group.

Flying groups

Some savanna birds live in huge groups. They fly in groups called **flocks**. These birds are quelas. A flying flock of quelas looks like a big, dark shape in the sky.

Life without rain

During the months when there is no rain, savannas are dry. There is no water or food for some animals. Many animals walk or fly to other habitats to find water and food. Wildebeests leave savannas for part of the year. They return to savannas when it rains there.

Digging in

Some animals stay in savannas all year. Monitor lizards stay all year. Monitor lizards drink and eat a lot when it rains. They do not need to drink or eat very much when it is dry.

Safe in savannas

Savanna animals have ways of staying safe from animals that eat them. Some animals can run very fast. Ostriches are fast runners. They race away from animals that chase them.

Safe babies

Many savanna carnivores eat baby animals. Carnivores can catch baby animals easily. Many adult animals protect their babies. Mother elephants always stay close to their babies.

Words to know and Index

animals
4, 5, 6, 18, 19, 20, 21, 22, 23, 24, 25, 26, 28, 29, 30, 31

energy
24-25

food
6, 14, 15, 18, 19, 20, 22, 23, 28

grasses
8, 12, 16, 17, 18, 20, 21, 23, 24

habitats
4-5, 6, 7, 8, 18, 28

plants
4, 5, 6, 12-13, 14, 15, 16, 17, 20, 21, 22, 23, 24

savannas
8, 9, 10, 11, 12, 13, 16, 17, 18, 20, 21, 22, 26, 27, 28, 29, 30, 31

water
5, 6, 11, 12, 13, 14, 15, 18, 28

Other index words

carnivores 21, 25, 31
herbivores 20, 22, 24
living things 5, 6, 14, 24
non-living things 5
omnivores 21, 22
photosynthesis 14

Printed in the U.S.A.